Bess M Thornton

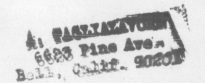

Public Speaking—

*As Listeners Like It!*

# Public Speaking—
# As Listeners Like It!

BY

## RICHARD C. BORDEN

*Author of "How to Deliver a Sales Presentation,"*
*Co-Author of "How to Win a Sales Argument,"*
*"Speech Correction," "The New*
*Public Speaking"*

HARPER & BROTHERS

NEW YORK AND LONDON

## DEDICATION

This book is dedicated to the near-sighted gentleman in the fifth row, who leans slightly forward in his seat as you step out onto the speaker's platform.

It is dedicated to—*your* listener.

# FOREWORD

THE principles in this text are formulated by the greatest living authority on public speaking—*the man who listens to you.*

All of the principles formulated by this authority have one important thing to recommend them.

They work!

If you apply these principles, your listeners will like you.

They will believe you.

They will understand you.

They will follow you.

And these listener responses *you must get.* Unless you get them, your speech is not a speech. It is a mere performance.

# CONTENTS

# LISTENERS' LAWS FOR SPEECH ORGANIZATION

## CHAPTER PURPOSE

THE fundamental law of speech organization can be stated in eight words:

Give every speech you make purpose—and form!

Listeners like vertebrate speeches—speeches with a *spine.*

They dislike speech jellyfish.

They dislike flabby, shapeless speeches that begin nowhere, ramble on in all directions—and end up in the air.

Chapter I presents a tested organization formula for each of the four major speech types:

1. The Formal Platform Speech
2. The Informal Conference-room Speech
3. The Speech of Introduction
4. The After-dinner Speech

All other speech types are but variants of these basic four.

# HOW TO ORGANIZE A FORMAL PLATFORM SPEECH THAT LISTENERS LIKE

## The Formal Platform Speech

THE organization formula of the formal platform speech is not complex. It is simple.

It is so simple that you can write it on your thumb nail:

1. Ho hum!
2. Why bring that up?
3. For instance!
4. So what?

The apparently cryptic phrases in this formula describe the four stages of audience reaction which you, as a platform speaker, must meet.

They are the clues to the four-step organization of your speech.

### First Step: Ho hum!

IN THE FIRST SECTION OF YOUR FORMAL PLATFORM SPEECH—START A FIRE!

Your speech is not well organized unless you kindle a quick flame of spontaneous interest *in your first sentence.*

3

Smokers do not like matches that fail to light with the first scratch. Listeners do not like speakers who fail to "light" with the first sentence.

When you rise to make a speech, do not picture your audience as waiting with eager eyes and bated breath to catch your message.

Picture it, instead, as definitely bored—and distinctly suspicious that you are going to make this situation worse.

Picture your listeners as looking uneasily at their watches, stifling yawns and giving vent to a unanimous "HO HUM!"

The first sentence of your speech, like the three redskins who bite the dust in the opening sentence of the Western thriller, must crash through your audience's initial apathy.

Don't open your speech on Safety First by saying: "The subject which has been assigned me is the reduction of traffic accidents." Say, instead: "Four hundred and fifty shiny new coffins were delivered to this city last Thursday."

Don't open your attack on installment buying with the sentence: "I would like to invite your attention tonight to the grave consequences which

4

may follow continuance of the installment plan psychology in buying." Say, instead: "Some of the people in this room suffer from a deadly disease—the disease of future chasing."

Emulate the technique of Henry Ward Beecher, as related by Milton MacKaye:[1]

> Henry Ward Beecher had a genius for bringing the most somnolent audience to life. One July morning he rode into a West Virginia town which was widely known in lecture circles as "Death Valley"—for the reason that any speaker unfortunate enough to have an engagement to lecture there wilted and curled up when he faced the town's stupid and indifferent audience.
>
> Beecher was duly warned. That afternoon, when he was being introduced, half the audience was already dozing. Beecher rose from his chair and, wiping his brow with a large handkerchief, strode to the front of the platform.
>
> "It's a God-damned hot day," the clergyman began.

[1] Published in *The New Yorker*.

5

A thousand pairs of eyes goggled and an electrical shock straightened the crowd erect. Beecher paused and then, raising a finger of solemn reproof, went on, "That's what I heard a man say here this afternoon!"

He proceeded into a stirring condemnation of blasphemy—and took his audience with him.

### Second Step: Why bring that up?

IN THE SECOND SECTION OF YOUR FORMAL PLATFORM SPEECH—BUILD A BRIDGE!

Your listener lives on an island—an island of *his* interests.

Why should he worry, for instance, about this jungle war between Bolivia and Paraguay, which you have introduced as the subject of your speech?

"Yes," your listener admits, "you caught my attention by an intriguing opening sentence. But in the cold light of second thought—*why bring up this subject anyway?*"

The second section of your speech must answer this question squarely.

"I bring up this subject of an apparently remote

6

war because the war in reality is not remote. It affects *your* morning cup of coffee. Through its influence on Latin-American trade it affects the number of dollars in *your* pocketbook. The repercussions of this war are rattling the furniture in *your* home."

Thus, in a few sentences, you build a bridge from the heart of a far-off jungle—to the little island of your listener's interests.

Listen to a psychologist motivate his talk on insanity before an audience of parents. He has introduced the subject of insanity with a ho-hum squelching opening sentence, but his listeners are now asking, "Why bring that up?"

I invite you parents to consider this subject of insanity, because *you* have most at stake.

*Your* child, today, has almost one chance in twenty of being confined to an asylum before he dies.

And suppose your child escapes? *You* are still affected.

If your neighbor's boy is the victim, records show that institutional life will claim him for

7

approximately seven years. The twenty-five thousand dollars expended by the state during those seven years, *you* will pay.

Whether as a parent, or as a taxpayer, *you* are vitally interested in this subject of insanity.

It makes no difference whether the subject of your speech is jungle warfare or insanity. In either case you must build a bridge to your listeners.

Until this bridge is built, you are not ready to begin the body of your speech.

### Third Step: For instance!

IN THE THIRD SECTION OF YOUR FORMAL PLATFORM SPEECH—GET DOWN TO CASES!

Let's assume that you have introduced your speech subject interestingly, arresting all ho-hums with your first sentence—that you have motivated it deftly, convincing your listeners in your second sentence that the subject hits their interests.

*Now get down to cases.*

The body of your speech must be keyed to one relentless audience demand—FOR INSTANCE!

To be true, the body of your speech properly

begins with some purposive general assertion about your subject. But once you have made this key assertion, resist the temptation to "put the idea in other words."

Your audience is not interested in "other words." It is tapping its collective foot impatiently and demanding—"FOR INSTANCE!"

If you start your speech body by asserting that wars are caused by economic rivalry, let your next sentence deal with the War of 1812, the Franco-Prussian War of 1870, the World War. *For instance!*

If you claim that modern advertising is dishonest, let your next sentence deal with tooth paste, corn plaster, memory-training courses, fat-reducers. *For instance!*

If you claim that the oil-burner you represent will change cellars into living-rooms, let your next sentence describe the glorified cellar of Mr. Davis, the cellar of Mrs. Wilkins, the cellar of the family next door. *For instance!*

Listen to Marcus Duffield who has just intro-duced and motivated the subject of overlapping functions in bureaus of the federal government. Note how he plunges immediately into his for-instances, after opening the body of his speech with a *purposive assertion* about his subject.[2]

> Overlapping functions in government bureaus are not necessary—but just plain foolish!
>
> Take highways. An ordinary public highway is built by the Bureau of Public Roads of the Department of Agriculture.
>
> If it runs through a national park, the National Park Service of the Department of the Interior builds it.
>
> If it is in Alaska, the Engineer Corps of the War Department builds it.
>
> Take colonial government. Hawaii is governed by the Department of the Interior; the Philippines by the War Department; Guam by the Navy Department.
>
> Take foxes. If a man shoots a fox in Alaska, he must settle accounts with the Department of Agriculture. But if he traps the

[2] Published in article form in *Vanity Fair*.

fox, he must settle with the Department of Commerce.

If you think two-department care of Alaskan foxes is just an accident—then take bears!

The Secretary of the Interior protects grizzly bears.

The Secretary of Commerce protects polar bears.

And the Secretary of Agriculture protects brown bears.

If a brown Kodiak bear has twins, one brown and one black, they are under the auspices of two different federal departments.

As you analyze the preceding speech excerpt, note that the speaker does not present his "for-instances" in a jig-saw jumble. He presents them as organized platoons—in marching order.

Note also that when one platoon marches by, that's the end of it. The speaker does not say, in the middle of his wild-life discussion: "Oh, by the way—while I was on the subject of highways, I should have mentioned . . ."

Remember this when you come to the body of *your* speech. *Listeners like speakers who serve their "for-instances" as course dinners, not goulash!*

## Fourth Step: So what?

IN THE CONCLUDING SECTION OF YOUR FORMAL PLATFORM SPEECH—ASK FOR ACTION!

The end of your speech, like the end of your pencil, should have a *point*.

The conclusion of your speech must be more than a graceful leave-taking. It must be more than a review of the for-instances covered in the body of your speech. It must be more than a reminder of your subject's general importance.

It must answer the audience's question: "SO WHAT?"

"So far, so good," say your listeners. "You have introduced your subject in a manner to arrest our attention. You have motivated it in a manner to command our serious interest. You have illustrated it with enough concrete cases to carry conviction. But now what? Where do we go from here? What do you want us to do about all this?"

In the conclusion of your speech, ask your audience for some specific action—some action response *which it is within their power to give.*

Join! Contribute! Vote! Write! Telegraph! Buy! Boycott! Enlist! Investigate! Acquit! Convict!

When you feel tempted to end your speech without such a request for action, remember the Chinese proverb of the Middle Ages:

"To talk much and arrive nowhere is the same as climbing a tree to catch a fish."

### Illustrations of Formal Platform Speeches That Listeners Like

In each of the following two-minute speeches, the Listener Formula for organizing a formal platform address is accurately applied.

As you read these illustrations, note, in passing, that much can be said in two minutes.

The world would be merrier, and listeners happier, if more speeches were only two minutes long.

### Illustration I

(Bruce Barton is urging an audience of young men to use their spare hours constructively.[8])

[8] Published in article form in *The American Magazine.*

*Ho hum!* Last month a man in Chicago refused a million dollars for an invention he had evolved *in his spare time.*

*Why bring that up?* You are interested in this because it confronts you with the possibilities of *your* spare time. Did you ever stop to think that most of the world's great men have achieved their true life work, not in the course of their needful occupations, but—*in their spare time?*

*For instance!* A tired-out rail-splitter crouched over his tattered books by candle-light or by fire-glow, at the day's end; preparing for his future, instead of snoring or skylarking like his co-laborers. Lincoln cut out his path to later immortality—*in his spare time.*

An underpaid and overworked telegraph clerk stole hours from sleep or from play, at night, trying to crystallize into realities certain fan-

14

tastic dreams in which he had faith. Today the whole world is benefiting by what Edison did—*in his spare time.*

A down-at-heel instructor in an obscure college varied the drudgery he hated by spending his evenings and holidays in tinkering with a queer device of his, at which his fellow teachers laughed. But he invented the telephone—*in his spare time.*

*So what?*  Gentlemen, you, too, have spare time. The man who says: "I would do such and such a great thing, if only I had time!" would do nothing if he had all the time on the calendar. There is always time—*spare time*—at the disposal of every human who has the energy to use it. USE IT!

*Illustration II*

(Floyd W. Parsons is urging
an audience of depression-dis-
couraged business men to face
the future with confidence.[4])

*Ho hum!* Fifty years ago an old gentleman
resigned from the Patent Office because he felt his job had no future;
he felt sure there was nothing more
to be invented.

*Why bring* A great many of us today, stand-
*that up?* ing in the shadow of the world depression, feel like that old man of
the Patent Office. For us, the wheels
of the world have creaked to a stop.
There is no future. Actually, *there
was never a time in all history when
the prosperity-creating forces of
science and invention were as active
as today!*

[4] Published in article-series form in *Advertising and Selling.*

*For instance!* The amazing new industry known as electronics has quickly developed into a billion-dollar business. The simple little electron tube will give us high-tension transmission by direct current over unprecedented distances—and will probably create, in power transmission alone, the need for tens of millions of dollars of additional equipment.

The infant plastics industry will eventually touch practically every other business. It means the production of millions of useful articles in huge quantities through the use of metal molds and hydraulic presses. These articles run all the way from pen barrels to steering-wheels—from buttons and lipstick-holders, to furniture and imitation marble.

The immediate future will witness a revolutionary development in the use of new materials and waste materials. The ocean will be made to

17

yield dozens of new values in the way of oils, iodine, glue, insulin, durable leather. The waste from woodworking plants will be converted into linoleum, toys, explosives, soap, chemicals, and artificial fibers. An acid valuable in paint and varnish industries will be extracted from the wax-like coating of apple peels. Farmers will grow licorice for insulation boards, cotton for stationery and potato-bags, cotton stalks for rayon, weeds for rubber, sweet potatoes for a tasteless stamp glue, corncobs and corn stalks for anæsthetics, perfumes, flavors, pulp.

*So what?* Gentlemen, it is a mistake for any of us to conclude that the world's work is done. Irresistible forces of invention are shaping a new prosperity. *Have faith in the future!*

# HOW TO ORGANIZE A CONFERENCE COMMENT THAT LISTENERS LIKE

# The Informal Conference-Room Speech

A SMALL deliberative group has assembled. The chairman raps sharply with his gavel.

"Gentlemen, you know the business of the meeting. A proposal has been made that our organization officially endorse the two-percent sales tax as a source of city revenue. What is your pleasure?"

A resolution is made and seconded that support be given, as proposed. Discussion becomes general. As a member of the conference group, you rise and ask for the floor:

"Mr. Chairman, I urge the defeat of the pending motion, because . . ."

Now what?

Does the speech you have begun obey the organization rules covered in the first chapter?

Not quite.

The informal conference-room speech differs from the formal platform speech both in its opening and in its conclusion. The conference comment must adapt itself to two special requirements of group discussion.

## REQUIREMENT NO. 1

Group discussion must secure the lively interaction of many minds. This is accomplished through speech sprints, not speech marathons.

## REQUIREMENT NO. 2

Group discussion must adhere to strict rules of relevance. The "lively interaction of many minds" results in action only when all discuss the same thing at the same time. The conference-room speaker cannot choose and motivate his own subject. His every comment must concentrate *on the exact issue under discussion at the moment he has the floor.*

To meet these special requirements of group discussion, observe the following five-step formula in organizing your conference comment.

### First Step:

*Decide on one specific reason why you are for or against the pending resolution.*

To be true, you may have several reasons—and all good ones, too.

But your first job in organizing a conference comment is to pick out *one*.

The brevity which conference listeners demand in every speaker requires thought unity.

Remember that in the conference situation there is no audience in the usual sense of the term. All are speakers. All want a chance for the floor.

The surest way to gain immediate audience dislike is to start your conference comment this way:

"Mr. Chairman, I oppose the proposed municipal sales tax for three reasons, which I shall consider seriatim."

By this time your listeners thoroughly resent you. You have branded yourself as a floor hog. And worse than that. By introducing three issues

22

at one time you have muddied the waters of discussion.

The way to get those three reasons of yours onto
the record is to get the floor three times. Make
three one-point speeches—all short.

Whatever you do, don't scramble all of your
reasons into one speech omelet. *Conference listeners don't like omelets!*

### Second Step:

*Condense the specific reason selected
for your conference comment into one
unforgettable sentence.*

It isn't easy to phrase a thought in an "unforgettable" sentence.

But it can be done!

Let's go back to that sales-tax speech of yours
and have a try.

"Even though the sales tax will give us the
funds which our city needs at the moment,
it is basically unsound as a tax principle—
and we should not forsake fundamental principle for momentary expediency"

How's that?

Terrible!

Your key-issue sentence is too long to remember. It's too complicated, grammatically. And it's too abstract. Try again:

> "The sales tax should be defeated on the grounds that expediency should not be permitted to defeat principle."

Your key-issue sentence this time is simpler and shorter. But it still isn't short enough. Words are like sunbeams; the more they are concentrated, the deeper they burn. That key-issue sentence of yours must burn more deeply into your audience's memory.

> "Don't give your vote to expediency—give it to principle!"

That's better. Your sentence is now down to the size of a ten-word telegram. But it's still abstract. It lacks sparkle. Listeners find it hard to remember a sentence in which they can *see* nothing. Who ever saw "expediency"? Who ever saw "principle"?

This time let's try some simple analogy that will convey the same idea, yet transform the abstract into the concrete.

"Don't sell the day to serve the hour!"

And there you have it!—a sentence which expresses the key idea of your conference comment *compactly, concretely,* and *unforgettably.*

But why go to all this trouble of carving out an epigram for each conference comment?

Because if you don't, your speech won't be remembered long enough to count. Only that conference comment counts which is remembered fifteen or twenty minutes after it is made—*when the vote is taken.*

You can't stick a piece of paper to the wall with mush. You need a thumb-tack.

A short, pointed, memorably phrased key-issue sentence is the thumb-tack with which you pin the idea of your conference comment into the wall of audience memory.

A sword without a sheath rusts. A good key-issue idea without a good key-issue sentence evaporates.

### Third Step:

*Use your key-issue sentence as your opening sentence.*

A good conference speaker opens his comment like a knife-thrower throws his knife—point first!

Conference-room listeners are not leisurely listeners. They are *executives* who have business on hand that they are anxious to get done.

"What do you want us to do with the pending resolution—and why?"

This is the question which your listeners ask the very second you rise to your feet. "WHAT? WHY?"

Don't delay your answer. If you delay it even a few sentences, you may get an unfavorable listener reaction. "Will he ever come to the point?" is an unuttered question which forms quickly in impatient minds.

Owen D. Young was once asked how he made such swift decisions.

"A man will come to your desk, Mr.

26

Young," said the questioner, "and present a fairly elaborate proposal. Instead of saying that you will take it under advisement for several weeks, you say Yes or No—and your swift decision is usually right. How do you do it?"

"When I tell you how I make those swift decisions," replied Mr. Young, "you may think that I am guided by an unreliable index—but I have found it's an index that works. I am guided very largely by the *first sentence* uttered by the man interviewing me.

"I have found from experience that if my interviewer doesn't thoroughly understand the proposal he is presenting, his first sentence will be confused.

"If he secretly doesn't believe in the proposal, his first sentence will be evasive.

"If the details of the proposal aren't concrete in his own mind, his first sentence will be abstract.

"On the other hand, a proposal that is opened by a sentence which is clear, compact, and concrete—*is usually worth-while.*"

27

If you would please not only the Owen D. Youngs in your audience, but all the other conference listeners who instinctively apply the same first-sentence test, start strongly.

Don't ooze into your speech. Begin point first—with your "thumb-tack" key-issue sentence.

### Fourth Step:

*Support your key-issue sentence with "for instances" that follow a straight line of relevance.*

In the body of your conference comment, illustrate only the *one point* which you have stressed in your opening sentence.

The temptation, of course, is to present whatever illustrations you happen to have in your possession, relevant or irrelevant. The temptation is to feed your idea baby not only milk, but peanuts and door knobs.

Resist this temptation!

The special conditions of group discussion demand strict relevance.

Having stated your key issue in your opening

sentence, stick to it like a burr. In your parade of "for-instances", *stay on Main Street!*

### Fifth Step:
*Repeat your key-issue sentence as your closing sentence.*

It is not enough that your conference comment open strongly.

It must close with equal strength.

Some time ago a famous chef was interviewed by a newspaper feature-writer. "Hard times," said the chef, "have forced me to build many an important banquet down to a price. But there is one thing I have never economized on—and never will. The coffee! *Because that's the taste people go away with.*"

Make sure the last sentence of your conference comment is not poor coffee. Make sure it is not a platitude—not a faltering confession that you have nothing more to say—not a soft-focus fade-out.

End strongly—by resounding the speech keynote with which you began.

## WHAT? WHY?

If you repeat your key-issue sentence in closing, you do more than end strongly. You give your conference comment a stylistic form—a wrapped-up effect—that listeners like.

And you do more than that.

You give your comment *persuasive impact*.

When you took part in a snowball fight as a boy, you usually didn't get hurt. Why? Because your opponents packed together loose fluffs of snow—just as speakers usually pack together loose fluffs of words.

But occasionally the tough boy from across the railroad tracks would get into the fight, and then things were different. He'd put a *rock* in the middle of his snowballs. When one of those rock snowballs hit you, you stayed hit!

The rock in the word snowball of your conference comment is your compact, concrete, forcefully worded key-issue sentence. If you use this sentence in both opening and closing, it will give your speech *persuasive impact*.

Your conference comment should be a two-bladed ax, with a sharp cutting edge at both ends.

### Illustrative Conference Comment

(A citizens' committee is considering support of a resolution which would make *all* crimes of violence punishable by death. A speaker rises to urge the adoption of this resolution).

| | |
|---|---|
| *Key issue opening* | Mr. Chairman, Gentlemen of the Conference, *Death for dealers of death is a policy that works!* |
| *Relevant for-instances* | At the close of the seventeenth century the English faced a crime wave far worse than ours. |

A trip from one English city to another, in those days, was a hazardous adventure. Some roads were so unsafe as to be literally impassable. Endless murders and robberies took place on the streets of London.

How did the English end this crime wave?

Not by calling in psychiatrists or theorists of moral uplift.

The English ended their crime wave by calling in Jack Ketch!

When a robber or murderer was caught, they turned him over to the hangman. Brutal? Yes—but it *worked*.

By the end of the century, criminal strains in England were largely stamped out, and the country has been notably free from crimes of violence ever since.

When the time comes for you to vote on the pending motion, Gentlemen, remember that we are not asking you to support an untried measure.

*Key issue closing* — *Death for dealers of death is a policy that works!*

Comment on Illustration:

Note in the preceding illustration that the speaker achieves brevity and unity by basing his conference comment on one key issue. He embodies this key issue in a "thumb-tack" sentence which is compact and sparkling. He leads with this sentence—crisply. He closes with it—strongly.

Note also that in the body of his speech, the speaker stays "on Main Street." He starts with a sharp point: "It works!" He ends with the same sharp point: "It works!" And in between, he observes Euclid's Law: A STRAIGHT LINE IS THE SHORTEST DISTANCE BETWEEN TWO POINTS.

# HOW TO ORGANIZE A SPEECH
# OF INTRODUCTION THAT
# LISTENERS LIKE

## The Speech of Introduction

LISTENERS are very definite in their concept of a good speech of introduction.

Here are some of the more important listener laws which you must remember when you are an introducer:

1. You must be brief.
2. You must avoid all stale and stilted phrases such as: "It is indeed a pleasure . . . a man who needs no introduction . . . we are gathered here tonight . . . "
3. You must avoid embarrassing the speaker by over-florid predictions of the treat that awaits the audience.
4. You must resist the temptation to exaggerate your speaker's qualifications.
5. You must avoid giving your speaker false starts. *E.g.* " . . . and so I take great pleasure in introducing Mr. John Johnson . . . [Mr. Johnson rises] . . . a man who is

eminently qualified in many ways . . ." (Mr. Johnson drops nervously back into his chair.)

6. Above all, you must avoid the sin of spotlight stealing. Your purpose as an introducer is *not* to steal thunder from the man you are presenting. Nor is it to give the audience a sample of what it is missing because the program committee did not have the good judgment to schedule you for the main speech as well as the speech of introduction.

Your purpose as an introducer is to help the speaker you are presenting to get off to a fast start —on the right foot.

The best way to accomplish this purpose is to answer four simple audience questions in organizing your speech of introduction. Answer them in the order given below. Answer them accurately, interestingly, *briefly.**

1. Why *this subject*?
2. Why this subject *before this audience*?

* How brief is brief? For the average speech of introduction— thirty seconds!

3. Why this subject before this audience *at this time?*

4. Why this subject before this audience at this time *by this speaker?*

If you answer these questions skillfully, the short prelude of your introduction will create a pleasant harmony between subject, audience, occasion, and speaker.

And now comes your critical moment as an introducer—the moment of presentation.

Handle this moment carefully. Make it a climax, not an inaudible afterthought.

As the last word of your last sentence, with a climactic intonation of unmistakable finality, announce your speaker's name. Announce it clearly and with sharply increased voice volume.

"Ladies and Gentlemen, I present to you [slight pause] Mr. JOHN JOHNSON!"

Continue to face your audience as you deliver this last sentence, in order that the speaker's name is not lost through a premature turn of the head.

Then swing swiftly about and face your speaker

with an alert expression of friendly welcome on your face.

Remain standing in this position until the speaker rises and acknowledges your introduction with a nod and the customary, "Mr. Chairman . . ."

Then sit down. Your work is done.

## Illustrative Speech of Introduction

(A student has the assignment of introducing Charles Edward Russell, speaking on "The New Industrial Era," to an annual meeting of the American Association of Manufacturers.)

*Why this subject?* Ladies and Gentlemen, the whole world today is craning its neck to peer around the corner. Will the "New Industrial Era" lead down— or up?

*Why this audience?* To the men in this room—manufacturers all—this question is doubly interesting.

*Why this occasion?* We are particularly interested in it right now—because the deepened shadow of world depression which hangs over this year's meeting seems to indicate that the old industrial era, as we knew it, may not return.

*Why this speaker?* In our interpreter of the "New Industrial Era" we are fortunate. He is a journalist, lecturer, author of many important books, citizen of the world.

I present to you a member of our special diplomatic mission to Russia, our Commissioner to Great Britain on Public Information, a member of the President's Industrial Commission—Mr. CHARLES EDWARD RUSSELL!

# HOW TO ORGANIZE AN AFTER-
DINNER SPEECH THAT
LISTENERS LIKE

# THE AFTER-DINNER SPEECH

THERE is little fundamental difference between the after-dinner speech and the formal platform speech.

Both should be based on the organization formula which recognizes the four audience reactions:

1. Ho hum!
2. Why bring that up?
3. For instance!
4. So what?

The only important distinguishing earmark of the after-dinner speech is its emphasized use of the humorous illustrative story.

The after-dinner situation is more convivial than the platform situation, more intimate, more informal.

After-dinner listeners want not merely to learn, but to laugh in the learning. They want a worthwhile message—but they want that worth-while message brightened with highlights of whimsicality.

This means that the specialized organization formula for the after-dinner speech deals largely with the use of humorous illustrative stories.

The humorous illustrative story is dangerous speech material. When it's good, it's very, very good, but when it's bad, it's awful. If you would avoid laughter misfires and backfires in the organization of your after-dinner speech, observe five simple principles.

### First Principle:

*Make sure that the humorous illustrative story which you use in your after-dinner speech actually IS illustrative.*

After-dinner listeners are not vaudeville listeners.

They dislike the speaker who turns out to be merely an amateur comedian. They dislike the purposeless "that-reminds-me" rambler.

"An after-dinner speaker," writes one critic, who apparently had heard too many amateur comedians, "may be defined as a man who eats a dinner he doesn't want, in order to get up and tell stories he doesn't remember, to listeners who have heard them already."

Make sure you never illustrate this definition!

When you face an after-dinner audience, first establish a serious theme, exactly as you would do in a formal platform speech.

Then illustrate your serious theme by a whimsical story which is so apt, so thoroughly illustrative, that it doesn't make much difference whether your audience laughs or not. If your listeners laugh, fine! But if they don't, no harm done! The story still stands on its own legs as a legitimate for-instance.

Contrast with this laugh independence the complete laugh dependence of the after-dinner speaker who drags in a story by the hind leg. The audience instantly realizes that the speaker is not illustrating a point, but telling a joke. Well, suppose the joke isn't as good as the speaker thinks—and the audience doesn't laugh. What then?

The speaker's plight is pitiful. The muscles in

his face work visibly to conceal his embarrassment. His Adam's apple jumps up and down.

Finally he says: "Well, I guess that wasn't so good. Let's see, where was I?" And he flounders on.

If your humorous story is really illustrative, however, a laugh misfire is not fatal. You have not failed to get a laugh. You have succeeded in illustrating your point interestingly.

A laugh in an after-dinner speech is a by-product. It is not a strained-for end in itself.

## Second Principle:

*Make the transition from your speech context into your humorous illustrative story—casually.*

"That reminds me of the story of the two Irishmen . . ."

"It seems there were once four Scotchmen . . ."

"In this connection I heard a good story last week . . ."

All such story-opening phrases are taboo! They *announce* that you are now about to tell a funny story. And the natural listener reaction is: "All right! Try and make me laugh. This had better be good!"

The good humorous story sneaks up on the listener and bites him in the leg when he isn't looking. It preserves the invaluable quality of surprise.

Get out of your speech context and into your story so casually that there is no dividing line. Throw the clutch without a noisy clashing of gears.

### Third Principle:

*Make the transition from your humorous illustrative story back into your speech context—purposively.*

"But to become serious again . . ."
"Let's see now, where was I? . . ."
"But to get back to the point . . ."

Such transition phrases are not transitions at all. They are thought jolts which make your listeners suspect, quite properly, that the story you have just completed was just so much digressive nonsense.

The last sentence of your story and the first sentence of your resumed speech context should mesh with an easy naturalness—with an "and-so-we-see" *purposiveness.*

### Fourth Principle:

*In your selection of a humorous illustrative story, avoid the laugh mechanism which is based on a pun.*

In the first place, the pun rarely gets the laugh you expect.

In the second place, even when you do get your laugh, there is present an unpleasant connotation of "wise-cracking" which after-dinner listeners dislike.

Play safe—and avoid the pun.

### Fifth Principle:

*Make sure that the humorous illustrative story which you choose for your after-dinner speech is one you can tell with practiced skill.*

The fact that some one else brought down the house with a certain story doesn't mean that your bungling attempt to retell it will get the same laugh.

Far from it!

A laugh depends, not on the story plot—but on its *telling*.

More than any other type of speech material, a humorous story demands in the telling both precision and economy in the use of words, fluency— and a masterly lightness of touch.

## Illustrative After-dinner Speech
## That Listeners Like

(Don Knowlton is addressing a banquet audience of advertising executives.[5] Note that he uses the four-step formula of the formal platform speech. The distinction of his address lies in a genial lightness of touch, not in an abandonment of purposiveness or form. Note also that the speaker gets into and out of his whimsical illustrative stories

[5] This illustration published in article form in *The Atlantic Monthly.*

*deftly.* There is no straining to drag in a joke, no dependence on "gag lines".)

*Ho hum!*  A magic phrase has elevated, overnight, peddler into preacher, "Truth in Advertising!"

*Why bring that up?*  I quote this sacred phrase of your profession because it's high time that some one asked, bluntly, "Who *wants* truth in advertising?"

You who demand the truth, have you not left in your souls one single shred of compassion? Have you ever known one man or woman in the world who had the courage to face stark truth?

*For instance!*  Would you have, for instance, "Truth in Democracy"? Then sharpen your pencil, censor, and we will start at the beginning.

That line, "All men are created equal," cross that out. That's almost as bad as "Not a cough in a carload."

48

Ah, here's a phrase which certainly must be deleted: "Government of the people, by the people, for the people." Some of these copywriters are brilliant fellows, you know, but they simply will not stick to facts.

Would you have "Truth in Religion"?

Let us revise the hymnal. It will not be so difficult. A sample page, for instance, might read like this:

We shall gather by the river,
    Where bright angel feet have trod;
With its crystal tide forever
    Flowing from the throne of God.

Then underneath the hymn we could put the footnote: "The statements contained in this hymn, while not guaranteed to be true, are based upon information which we believe reliable."

Would you have "Truth in Behavior"?

Rule out "I'm pleased to meet you" at once. Sincerity is the keynote. Exclaim, "I loathe the sight of you and I hope you choke!"

Never say, "Oh, must you go so soon?" Just shout, "Hooray!" and kick your guests out jovially, with the aid of a lead pipe. At bridge, strangle your partner. Copy-edit from your vocabulary "We've had a marvelous time." Tell your host the truth and kick him in the shins by way of emphasis.

If we don't want truth in democracy, religion, or behavior, why should we want it in advertising?

Minnie Schultz sits on her attic cot, surveying her bulging calves. For her face she knows there is no hope, but love does not stop at the chin. If only that excess ninety pounds . . .

Ah! It says in the paper, "Take Madam Maloney's curious concoction for three weeks, and flesh will fall from you like leaves in October, revealing the lithe limbs in all their pristine elegance. Only fifty cents a bottle . . ."

Fifty cents for romance! Fifty cents for love! Fifty cents to tread the path of Guinevere, to emulate the exploits of Cleopatra. Who could begrudge the spending of that 5c cents?

Consider Abner Snodgrass. He is not a happy man. He knows not whether it is the presence of B.O. or the absence of S.A. but the fact remains that women observe him never.

Then comes the cheering message: "They laughed at me when I sat down at the piano. But within an instant the room was filled with awe. They could not believe I had learned to play in ten lessons—all by mail—"

Thirteen dollars and seventy-nine cents, and Mamie will make eyes at me. Ten short weeks, and Lucy will be jealous!

You truth-mongers, would you forbid this Caliban to become an Orpheus? Would you chide the ingenious satirist who collects $13.79 that this clod may catch for an instant the illusion of self-esteem?

*So what?*  No! Let us thank advertising that there is still alive in the world a champion of glorious illusion. The advertising sloganeers who painfully grind out their alliterative grist little know that the only true things which exist, in the minds of thousands, are the very illusions which this grist creates. *May they continue as they are*—for if they should speak the truth, then indeed "This is the end of every man's desire."

## CHAPTER II

# LISTENERS' LAWS FOR SPEECH SUBSTANCE

## CHAPTER PURPOSE

IN THE preceding chapter on speech architecture, you learned a two-word formula for investing the body of a speech with audience interest.

This two-word formula is so potent that it applies to the body of *all* speeches—the formal platform speech, the informal conference speech, the speech of introduction, and the after-dinner speech.

So magic are the two words in this formula, that if you repeat them about once every ten sentences, the body of every speech you make *must* be interesting.

These two words are—FOR INSTANCE!

Of course, if you apply this formula without adequate preparation, you will get into trouble. About the third time you say "For instance," you may clap your hand to your head and ask, "For instance—*what?*"

If the answer is "For instance—*nothing!*" the body of your speech has come to an end. Do not try to draw it out by abstract speculation, by unsupported assertion, or by mere repetitious wordiness. *The body of your speech has come to an end.*

No amount of speech organization can make up for lack of speech substance. No amount of manner can make up for matter.

The relationship between speech organization and speech substance is the relationship between cooking and food. When one of the early Puritan fathers wrote a recipe for cooking wild turkey, he quite properly began his instructions with the simple phrase, "First catch your turkey."

This is the basic listener's law governing speech substance. *First catch your "for-instances!"*

In this chapter you will learn the six forms of speech substance best adapted for the body of your speech—the six "for-instances" that listeners like best.

## 1. Listeners like "for-instances" in story form.

Listeners not merely *like* "for-instances" in story form. They *demand* them.

Until you learn how to animate the illustrations in the body of your speech with the narrative touch, you will remain "just another speaker."

Analyze yourself for a moment, not as a speaker, but as a listener. *What was the first listener demand that you ever put into words?* You were only a child when you voiced it—"Tell me a story!"

In the illustration that follows, an educator is urging an audience of parents to substitute psychology for the birch rod in the training of children. Note that he achieves not merely interest—but clarity as well—by using "for-instances" in story form.

Ladies and Gentlemen, the birch rod of "Don't! Don't!" is a poor child-trainer. A positive psychological appeal is a much more effective weapon.

Take, for instance, the case of Tommy. Tommy was a neighborhood pest who continually trespassed on flower-beds. Did his mother negatively insist, "You mustn't"? No. Tommy's mother did something much more effective. She gave the youngster a little plot in the back yard for a garden of his own. His interest once aroused, Tommy carefully dug up his tiny garden and planted seeds. He soon became enthusiastic over the sprouting seedlings—and woe to the careless feet that trespassed on *his* garden. Once he became a property-owner himself, he began to respect the rights of others.

Take, again, the case of Billy, aged ten. Billy just didn't seem able to resist taking things that belonged to others. His teacher reached—not for a birch rod—but for a positive appeal. "Billy," she said one day, "here's a list—and my purse. I want you to go to the store and do my shopping for me." When Billy asked if the teacher really meant that he was to carry her purse, she replied: "Certainly! You're the best arithmetic student in the class, and you can shop as well as I." When Billy returned, he offered to count the change—but his teacher told him that she knew it was correct. Each day the teacher found something similar for Billy to do. She sent him to the bank to deposit a check. And each time she commented on his trustworthiness to the class. This positive appeal to his pride soon made Billy one of the most trusted students in the class.

## 2. Listeners like "for-instances" which involve famous people.

If your story-form "for-instance" involves a famous person, its interest is measurably increased.

Even though the stories about Tommy and Billy in the preceding illustration were interesting, they would have been *more* interesting had they involved Tommy Edison—and Billy Shakespeare.

This is something you should note carefully!

Good stories involving famous people, with an illustrative angle that makes them useful to speakers, are not picked up overnight. *You must accumulate them*—slowly, systematically.

Listen to a preacher urge his audience to inject more simple kindliness into their daily lives:

Are you, perhaps, too busy to be kind?

According to Francis Jehl, Thomas Edison wasn't. One autumn day, the gray-haired inventor wandered about the grounds adjacent to his Menlo Park laboratories, busily engaged in a mental grapple with a scientific problem that called for complete concentration.

But as Edison walked on, head bowed in reflection, his steps brought him into the shadow of an old hemlock tree. Suddenly he stopped. His eyes focused on a tiny object before him. There, underneath the hemlock tree, fluttered a crippled bird, which apparently had been unable to join the autumnal caravan to the southlands.

Edison promptly forgot that he was "busy." He captured the bird and arranged for its care. After a time the bird showed a decided improvement and indicated a readiness for flight. But the kind saviour was doubtful about the bird's ability to meet the demands of the long air journey.

So what did Edison do—in the midst of his experiments? He made a comfortable little box, replete with such facilities as the frail passenger would require. He placed his little friend in the box, labeled it for a destination in South America—and delivered it to the express company with instructions to release the bird at the end of its journey.

Remember—Edison was a busy man.

But he wasn't too busy to find time for an act of simple kindliness.

In the preceding speech excerpt, the speaker effectively unites listener interest in stories with listener interest in famous persons.

Listen to Ray Giles employ the same technique as he urges an audience of business men to adopt a certain formula of success.

If you would be successful, always be willing to attempt the impossible.

Out in California, some years ago, an impatient fruit-grower was visiting one nursery after another to secure 20,000 prune trees. As though the order itself were not staggering enough, he required that the trees be delivered ready for planting within ten months.

"Impossible!" said one nurseryman after another. But Luther Burbank heard about the order and went after it.

The prune trees had to be started immediately, but prunes wouldn't sprout at that time of year. To make a beginning, Burbank planted almonds, which *could* be started then. He had to cover the germinated almonds with cloth, and as they poked their green spikes above the earth, he had to remove them, one at a time, to nursery rows.

When the young almond trees were well along, he grafted 20,000 prune buds into them.

In less than seven months Burbank delivered 19,025 prune trees ready for planting.

Gentlemen, if you would be successful, emulate Burbank's example. *Always be willing to attempt the impossible.*

### 3. Listeners like "for-instances" which animate the pages of history.

If your story-form "for-instance" dramatizes an incident of recorded history, it carries a persuasive weight which undocumented anecdotes often lack.

Stories about Tommy and Billy are usually regarded as "just stories," useful in the interests of exposition, but having no value as evidence.

Even stories about famous people are often accepted as George Washington-and-the-cherry-tree yarns.

But historical "for-instances" can *convince.*

In the following illustration, Arthur D. Little urges an audience to be tolerant of all new ideas —to examine them, unprejudiced by past traditions or present opinions.[1]

If you permit your opinions to harden, you retard your own advance, and you do something far worse. You retard the advance of the world.

There hangs in my office a picture entitled "The Arrest of Lavoisier." The great chemist, one of the greatest men ever produced by France, had been the first to explain combustion in the terms we now accept. During the French Revolution Marat denounced him as the "Master of Charlatans." In my picture Lavoisier listens in silent dignity to the reading of the warrant by an arrogant fellow in a red cap, behind whom crowds the exulting rabble. His arrest was followed by sentence of death from a judge who declared, "The Republic has no need of chemists."

Marco Polo, the greatest, and probably the

[1] This illustration published in article form in *The Technology Review*.

most accurate of mediæval travelers, returned to Venice from his amazing journey across the deserts of Persia to the dazzling court of the Great Khan—only to be greeted with incredulity and to acquire the insulting sobriquet of *Marco millioni*, Marco of the Millions. His story, which has since been verified in most of its details, was incredible. Who could believe in such things as paper money, printed books, black stones which burned, and nuts as large as a man's head? For many years after his return every carnival of Venice was enlivened by the preposterous antics of a clown who impersonated *Marco millioni*.

We are now living in what we call the machine age, and our civilization is largely based on coal and oil. Such foundation was not established nor was the machine developed without passionate resistance from people with hardened opinions. In the days of King Edward I, it was a capital offense to burn coal in London. In 1619 the growing scarcity of wood in England led Dudley

to attempt the substitution of coal for char-
coal in his blast furnace. The ironmasters
drove him out of Worcester County. He set
up another furnace. A riot was organized and
the furnace wrecked. Only 150 years ago today it was illegal to sell coal in the city of
Philadelphia.

Our gigantic petroleum industry came into
being because a man had faith in an idea at
which his neighbors scoffed. Edwin L. Drake,
of Titusville, Pennsylvania, believed that
large quantities of petroleum existed in sub-
terranean cavities. In 1859 he started drill-
ing, and his effort became the laughing-stock
of all western Pennsylvania. But when his
well filled with oil, Drake's folly became,
overnight, the envy of the countryside.

In 1802 William Murdoch made gas from
coal, and with it lighted his house in Corn-
wall. Furious opposition was aroused when
Murdoch and his associates attempted to ex-
tend the use of gas. Scott, Byron, and Napoleon were among those who ridiculed the
crazy notion. Scott wrote: "There is a mad-

man proposing to light the streets with—
what do you suppose—*smoke!*"

Don't let the arteries of *your* opinion
harden. The world moves irresistibly on.
Move with it!

In the preceding speech excerpt, Mr. Little
does more than interest his audience. He does
more than make his point clear. He wins *conviction* as well, through the use of story-form "for-
instances" that animate the pages of recorded
history.

### 4. Listeners like "for-instances" based on colorful analogies.

You should be glad to know that listeners like
"for-instances" based on analogies, because analogies, as a rule, are *your most effective weapons
of exposition*.

Do you remember how Luther Burbank grafted
his prune buds, that *wouldn't* grow, into almond
trees, that *would* grow?

That's the technique of clear explanation!

Graft the new idea, which your listeners don't

understand, into an old idea, which they do understand.

Suppose you are making a speech against monetary inflation. How will you explain to your listeners the nature of inflation? By abstract definition? By citing the technical expositions of economists?

Not if you are wise.

If you are wise, you will use a Burbank technique and proceed with your explanation as follows:

> There was once a farmer whose harvest yielded him 1,000 bushel baskets full of wheat.
>
> But he decided that this amount wasn't enough.
>
> So he placed an order for some smaller baskets.
>
> A week later the farmer smiled happily as he surveyed his inflated harvest. He now had 2,000 baskets full of wheat—2,000 *half*-bushel baskets.
>
> Ladies and Gentleman, you cannot add to

the wealth of a nation by changing the size of the tickets called money any more than you can create more wheat by reducing the size of bushel baskets.

Listen to John T. Flynn urge an audience to shun the stock market.

If you think you can dabble in the stock market and thus feather your nest, you will soon discover that you will not only go without feathers—but will probably lose the nest.

Speculation is a game more intricate than bridge. You wouldn't play bridge for a cent a point with the Culbertsons, would you? Well, in speculation you will be opposed by players at least as expert as the Culbertsons. Your opponents will furnish the deck, do all the dealing, will know their cards *and yours.*

Whenever you are confronted by a difficult task of exposition, use analogy-form "for-instances." Graft inflated dollars into bushel baskets, cross stock speculation with a bridge game.

### 5. Listeners like "for-instances" which dramatize important statistics.

"Our jails today are filled largely by aliens— who haven't bothered to apply for citizenship papers!"

So exclaims a speaker, arguing for the whole-sale deportation of alien criminals.

What is the quickest way to prove such a statement?

By analogy? By illustrative stories or anecdotes? By animating the pages of past history?

No.

To prove such a statement you must count noses.

It is often impossible for you to avoid the introduction of statistics into the substance of your speech.

And why *should* you avoid statistics?

Some place or other you've picked up the notion that figures bore listeners.

But that's where you're wrong.

Listeners *like* figure "for-instances"—

(1) if they are really important

(2) if they are easy to understand
(3) *if they are properly dramatized*

Note that in the following anti-war speech by Nicholas Murray Butler, statistics become more than a necessary evil in a process of proof. They are made a tool of *interest* as well as of persuasion.

> The money spent by all nations for the destructive purposes of the World War amounted to four hundred billion dollars.
>
> Do you know what we could have done with that money if we had used it constructively?
>
> We could have built a $2,500 house, furnished it with $1,000 worth of furniture, placed it in the middle of five acres of land worth $100 an acre, and given this estate outright to each and every family in the United States, Canada, Australia, Wales, Ireland, Scotland, France, Belgium, Germany, and Russia.
>
> We could have given to each city of 20,000 inhabitants or over, in each country named,

a five-million-dollar library and a ten-million-dollar university.

Out of what was left we could have set aside a sum at five per cent that would provide a $1,000 yearly salary for an army of 125,000 nurses, and another army of 125,000 teachers.

Who says statistics are inherently uninteresting? If you dramatize them, as Nicholas Murray Butler did in the preceding speech, they can be made to sparkle with interest.

It is even possible to use a narrative technique in the presentation of statistics. Note how this is done by a speaker arguing for municipal lotteries:

A municipal lottery will give us our first really popular basis for taxation.

*People will cheerfully stand in line for the privilege of being taxed.* If you don't believe it, listen to the speed-of-sale figures recorded by statisticians on the day the 1933 French National Lottery tickets were distributed.

Bong!

A bell marks the hour of eight and mists still partially obscure the streets of Paris.

But promptly at eight, the opening hour of the lottery sale, every tobacco-shop in the city is besieged by enthusiastic taxpayers. Hundreds of thousands of lottery tickets go like hot cakes. By 8:30 A.M., one-half hour after their stores opened, the tobacco dealers have exhausted their supply!

The Banque de France—opening at 9—runs through its supply in fifteen minutes. By 9:15 disappointed would-be taxpayers are racing elsewhere in their search for tickets.

Before the office of the national tax commissioner, who has a few hundred thousand tickets for distribution, stretches a long line. The line is composed of men and women who have sat up half the night on camp chairs. They have breakfasted on coffee brought to them in buckets by their families!

Gentlemen, these figures indicate that taxation based on municipal lotteries is popular.

## 6. Listeners like "for-instances" interwoven with visual aids.

The eyes of your listener are more learned than his ears.

Appeal to them as often as possible!

Use "for-instances" which can be made more vivid by the interweaving of simple visual aids.

If you are urging an audience to stay away from auction sales, pull out your watch and hold it up. Then ask: "Can you tell me the exact value of the watch which I hold in my hand? Look at it closely. Is it worth one hundred and twenty dollars—or a dollar and twenty cents? Do you KNOW? If you don't know, and know for certain, *you've no business at an auction sale!*"

Listen to a popular science lecturer explain to his listeners the growing importance of the photo-electric cell:

This tube [*holds up an "electric eye"*] is a tube that thinks. Only last week it caught a burglar. Picture the scene. It is late at night. The window of a private home in Boston opens. A marauder enters. His shadowy figure intercepts a beam of invisible ultra-violet light in front of a wall safe. A flashlight flares. A camera snaps a photograph of the intruder. Tear-gas volleys out—and the thug drops helplessly to the floor. Ten minutes later the police arrive.

The electric eye does more than catch burglars. It helped put this cigar in my pocket [*pulls out cigar from breast pocket*]. The top layer in a good box of Corona Coronas must contain only cigars of a uniform hue. Tobacco of the same color is now picked out for cigars by photo-electric cells which work faster and more efficiently than human eyes.

The photo-electric cell helped match the shades of color in my necktie [*pulls necktie out of vest*]. Delicate shades of cloth and dyes are matched by a tube which picks out variations of color that the human eye cannot even see.

Even the evening newspaper which I

bought on my way to this meeting [*holds up a newspaper*] owes a debt to the electric eye. Many newspaper presses are equipped with photo-electric cells which stop them if the paper breaks. Light directed upward from beneath the paper feeding into the press strikes an electric eye if the paper breaks.

# LISTENERS' LAWS FOR SPEECH PHRASEOLOGY

## CHAPTER PURPOSE

IN CHAPTER I you learned how to organize your speech thoughts *purposively*.

In Chapter II you learned how to illustrate your speech thoughts *effectively*.

In Chapter III you will learn how to phrase your purposively organized and effectively illustrated thoughts —*pleasingly*.

To be "pleasing" in your speech phraseology means more than you think.

It means that your language must be unvaryingly sincere. It means that your choice of words must reflect listeners' preference for the specific, the colorful, the picturesque. It means that your sentences must not only stand on their own grammatical legs, but must mesh coherently with their neighbors. It means, above all, that your phraseology must be unremittingly clear, expressing at all times your acceptance of the fundamental axiom that the purpose of language is to reveal thought, not to conceal it.

Your speech phraseology will be pleasing if you apply the six listener laws presented in this chapter.

### 1. Listeners like speech phraseology free from wax.

In ancient days Roman sculptors sometimes sought to conceal surface cracks in a statue with the aid of melted beeswax.

A buyer, deceived into believing that he was purchasing a flawless piece of marble, would place such a statue proudly in his atrium.

A few weeks later the beeswax would dry out, crumble away, and leave the original cracks exposed.

To such alarming proportions did this practice of wax trickery grow, it finally became the custom of reputable sculptors to guarantee their works as *sine cera*—literally translated, "without wax."

Our present word "sincere" we owe to a rebellion against wax.

You are not in the business of carving statues out of marble. But you do something basically similar. You carve speeches out of words.

*Beware the use of wax!*

Beeswax tricked the ancient Romans. But word wax never tricked anybody. It is instantly recognized and thoroughly despised by all listeners.

Word wax may be defined as any phrase, any group of words, which is not an *integral part* of the thought you seek to express.

For instance—

**(a)** *Superlatives are usually wax.*

"This is absolutely and positively essential!"

Eliminate the word wax and what remains is not less, but more forceful. "This is essential!"

"This is true beyond any possible shadow of a doubt!"

If you wish to strengthen the simple assertion, "This is true!" do so by presenting confirming "for-instances"—not by pouring word wax into the cracks.

**(b)** *Trite expressions are wax.*

When the introducer says, "We have in our midst . . . a man who needs no introduction . . . it is indeed an honor and a privilege . . . ", listeners mutter to themselves: "Word wax!"

When the graduation day speaker says, "As I look into your smiling faces . . ."

When the political orator shouts, "I believe I can say without fear of contradiction . . ."

When the conference-room debater asserts that his proposal will benefit "each and every man, woman and child throughout the length and breadth of the land . . ."

When any of these stale phrases assail the ears of listeners, a thumbs-down diagnosis is instantly made. *Word wax.*

(c) *Groping expressions are wax.*

"What I'm trying to get at is . . ."

"What I want to say is . . ."

If you want to get at something, then get at it!

If you want to say something, say it!

Your failure to express your idea clearly the first time is not helped by word wax. Try a "for-instance" instead.

(d) *Repetitious expressions are wax.*

"As I said before . . ."

77

"And so may I again repeat . . ."

If you wish to gain the emphasis which comes from restatement—as you do in the opening and close of a conference comment —go ahead and restate.

But omit the waxy "as I said before."

(e) *"And so forth" expressions are wax.*

"America has produced such inventors as Fulton, Edison, the Wright brothers—and so forth and so on."

When you list items in series, stop cleanly with your last item.

"And so forth" expressions are uncharitably interpreted as wax calculated to make others believe you know more than you do.

Such expressions have the same value as the obnoxious phrase, "I could go on this way for hours."

(f) *Weasel words are wax.*

"Of course it's only my opinion, but . . ."
"It seems to me . . ."

Of course it's your opinion! That's why you're expressing it.

Naturally "it seems to you," or you wouldn't be saying it.

"More or less . . . to a greater or less degree . . . or something like that . . ."

Punch-pulling phrases, which fuzz the crispness of a thought, are just as obnoxious as the superlatives at the opposite extreme.

Avoid them!

## 2. Listeners like speech phraseology that is grammatically sure-footed.

It often happens that you are called upon to deliver a speech extemporaneously.

This means that you have a chance to plan your speech organization and to select, mentally, a few good "for-instances." But there is no opportunity to plan a definite sequence of words.

This means that the extemporaneous-speaking situation submits to the acid test your ability to phrase your thoughts under fire—*grammatically*.

How easy it is to bog down in the middle of a sentence!

How easy it is to match plural subjects with singular verbs, to disrupt the form of a sentence with a shapeless parenthetical remark, to leave clauses hanging forlornly in the air!

But there is one simple way to keep out of trouble.

*Use plenty of periods.*

When a sentence begins to crumple under its own weight—period!

When a dependent clause starts to miss on one grammatical cylinder—period!

Short sentences are the royal highroad to grammatical surefootedness in extemporaneous speaking.

### Illustration I

(Lincoln Steffens is urging parents to animate their children with the pioneer spirit. Note that by a technique of short sentences he achieves not merely grammatical surefootedness, but *force.*[1])

Nothing is done.

Everything in the world remains to be done —or done over.

The greatest picture is not yet painted. The

[1] Published in article form in *The Cosmopolitan Magazine.*

greatest play isn't written. The greatest poem is unsung.

There isn't in all the world a perfect railroad. Nor a good government. Nor a sound law.

Physics and mathematics are being fundamentally revised. Chemistry is just becoming a science. Psychology, sociology, and economics await a Darwin.

Tell that to your children.

A faucet leaks. I cannot close it tight. Good. I call my seven-year-old son. He seizes the faucet, tries to turn it off. Can't. He grins.

"What's the matter, Pete?" I ask.

He looks up happily and gives the answer. "Grown-ups, Daddy."

Propaganda, of course. I have taught him that we, his elders, cannot make a fit faucet. And *he* may. There's a job for him and his generation in the plumbing business. And in every other business.

Teach *your* children—

That nothing is done, finally and right.

That nothing is known, positively and completely.

That the world is theirs . . . all of it!

## Illustration II

(Clarence Darrow, who always speaks extemporaneously, is addressing a jury in defense of "Big Bill" Haywood, the socialist leader. Haywood is on trial for the murder of ex-Governor Steunenberg of Idaho. Note that an important secret of Darrow's impromptu skill is the grammatical surefootedness which he achieves through short sentences.)

I want to speak to you plainly.

Bill Haywood is not my greatest concern.

Other men have died before him. Other men have been martyrs. They have met their death and Haywood can meet his. . . .

If you say he must.

If you kill him, your act will be applauded by many. In our great cities frock-coated men of means will speak well of you. Among the spiders and vultures of Wall Street will go up pæans of praise.

82

But if you free him, there are still those to thank you.

Simple men who will reverently bow their heads in gratitude.

Out on the broad plains where men toil with their hands.

Through our mills and mines and factories.

Down deep under the earth.

Men who suffer . . . women and children weary with toil . . . will kneel tonight and ask God to guide your judgments. . . .

*To save Haywood's life!*

## 3. Listeners like speech phraseology with good connective tissue.

"And . . . and . . . and . . ."

Why connect all your sentences with one weak overworked conjunction?

Don't treat sentences like strung sausages. Button some together. Try a hook and eye with others. Experiment with the zipper fastening. Develop skill with the square knot and the half-hitch.

The English language is rich with connectives

that express all shades of causal relationship, of subordination and climax, of time and place sequence.

> Notwithstanding . . .
> Consequently . . .
> In view of . . .
> Since . . .
> After all . . .
> Instead . . .
> Gradually . . .
> Despite . . .
> Soon . . .
> As a result . . .
> Climaxing . . .

Transfer connectives such as these from your passive vocabulary of understanding to your active vocabulary of *use*.

Your sentences, remember, must not merely stand on their own grammatical legs; they must help their neighbors.

### 4. Listeners like speech phraseology that is conversational.

Beware sounding like a book when you speak.

Your function as a speaker is to be communicative, not oracular.

You are not an essayist in an ivory tower, but a *man talking*. A man who talks his listener's language!

This does not mean that the phraseology of your speech should be mediocre or casual.

It *does* mean that your phraseology should achieve the sincere directness of conversation. Brilliant conversation! Organized conversation! Purposive conversation! But still—*conversation*.

To achieve the conversational touch, employ grammatical contractions such as "Wouldn't you . . .", "Doesn't it seem to you . . .", "Haven't you ever. . . ."

Above all—feature the second personal pronoun.

Freckle your phraseology with "you's!"

## 5. Listeners like speech phraseology that is specific.

Which is more interesting—

He passed between two trees.

Or—

He passed between a shagbark hickory and a stunted blue spruce.

The specific is *always* more interesting.

If you would develop the kind of phraseology that listeners like, talk of cucumbers rather than vegetables . . . of Frenchmen rather than foreigners . . . of eighty-mile-an-hour tanks rather than modern military equipment.

As the "for-instance" principle should guide you in planning ideas within the framework of your speech organization, so this same master principle should guide you in planning words within the framework of your speech phraseology.

Choose words which are *specific*!

Choose words so specific that they throw sharp shadows of individuality . . . words so specific that they have color . . . words so specific that your listeners *see* at the moment they hear.

If you are pleading for disarmament, don't say, "The safest nations in the world today are the unarmed countries."

Say, instead, "The safest nations in the world

today are the Swedens, the Norways, the Switzerlands, the Denmarks."

### 6. Listeners like speech phraseology
### that is picturesque.

The surest way to develop a colorful, picturesque manner of expression is to experiment with metaphors and similes.

For instance! How picturesque is the metaphor-bristling phraseology of Ralph Waldo Emerson as he discusses with his listeners "The Language of the Street":

> The language of the street is always *strong*.
> I confess to some pleasure from the *stinging* rhetoric of a *rattling* oath in the mouths of truckmen and teamsters. How *laconic* and *brisk* it is by the side of a page of the North American Review.
> *Cut these words of the street and they bleed; they are vascular and alive; they walk and they run.*
> Moreover, they who use them do not *trip* in their speech. Their phraseology is a

87

*shower of bullets*, whilst Cambridge men and Yale men correct themselves and begin again at every half sentence.

You can make the phraseology of your next speech as picturesque as Emerson's by using the same technique. Metaphors. Similes. Nouns that bleed. Verbs that sting and rattle.

### 7. Listeners like speech phraseology that is clear.

Clarity in your language takes precedence over every other listener demand.

Why, then, is it listed last in this chapter?

Because clarity is not a means—but an end.

It is the joint product of all the other elements in good speech phraseology.

It results from the sincerity of language free from word wax . . . from the simplicity of short sentences . . . from the coherence of good connective tissue . . . from the directness of the conversational style . . . from the exactness of specific words . . . from the picturesque vividness of metaphors and analogies.

If your speech phraseology is clear, you gain more than clarity. *To be clear is also to be convincing.*

The editors of the Encyclopædia Britannica appreciate this truth when they write:

> Nine readers out of ten take a lucid statement for a true one.

Napoleon knew his listeners' laws when he gave three instructions to the secretaries who relayed his messages:

Be clear!
Be clear!
Be clear!

## CHAPTER IV

# LISTENERS' LAWS FOR SPEECH DELIVERY

## CHAPTER PURPOSE

WHEN a good baseball pitcher delivers a ball, he does not deliver with his fingers alone.

He delivers with his arm, his shoulders, the muscles of his abdomen, his legs—and his brain.

The good speaker does not deliver with his voice alone.

He delivers with his body, his hands, his face, his eyes, his emotions, his intellect.

This is the master law of good delivery:

*Deliver with the full resources of your personality. Deliver both to your listener's ears—and to his eyes!*

This chapter gives you seven basic principles which will enable you to please your listener's eyes—and four basic principles which will enable you to please his ears.

# HOW TO PLEASE YOUR
# LISTENERS' EYES

## 1. Look at your listeners.

WHY should your listeners want you to look at them?

Because they are normally vain human beings, who appreciate having their presence acknowledged.

More than that!

*Listeners like to feel they are influencing what you say.*

If you look at them, they have a chance to signal you their reactions through nods of assent, frowns of disagreement, smiles of encouragement, lifted eyebrows of skepticism, expressions of boredom, forward leanings of interest.

The speaking situation then becomes an exciting two-way movement of thought. Your eye contact has transformed your audience from dead spectators into live participators. Your listeners are not on the side lines. *They are in the game!*

Dr. Flexner reports an interesting item from Russia:

The peasants in a certain Russian village were informed that the government proposed to install a radio so that they might hear the speeches made in Moscow. They promptly asked, "Can we talk back?"

When they received a negative answer they replied that on those terms *they did not care for the radio.*

Your listeners are like those Russian peasants. Look at them—so that they may have the satisfaction of "talking back."

A doorbell doesn't ring until you press a button that establishes electrical contact. An audience doesn't respond until you, as a speaker, press the button of eye contact.

Avoid dead doorbells and dead audiences.

Let your first thought as a speaker be the first thought of an aviator when he starts his plane:

## "CONTACT!"

### 2. Look at your listeners all the time.

Eye contact is most important *in the pinches,* during those long moments when you wrack your brain for a word or a thought that has escaped you.

If you continue to look at your audience during these moments of crisis, your listeners will appreciate your pause as part of your speech. "Just look at this man *think!*" they say to themselves. "Here is no glib babbler, but a speaker who really weighs his words."

How different is the audience reaction when your pause for thought is accompanied by a break in contact! "Aha!" reason your listeners. "This poor fellow has forgotten what he wanted to say. At the moment, he's afraid even to look at us."

When you sheepishly drop your eyes to the floor, *you walk out on your audience!* You transform a legitimate pause for reflection into a confidence-destroying signal of confusion.

By observing one simple rule, you can make your enforced pauses assets rather than liabilities:

Look at your audience *all* the time!

### 3. Look at all your listeners.

There are listeners in the front row. Look down at them now and then.

There is a chairman on the platform behind you. Swing around occasionally and address a few words to him.

And how about those listeners in the extreme right wing of the auditorium? Walk over to the edge of the platform and establish a more intimate contact with this group.

Then move over to the opposite side of the platform, where you can study more closely the left wing of your audience.

Don't forget those listeners in the galleries, either, nor those who are craning their necks to see you, away back in the rear.

*Distribution* of contact is as important as its maintenance.

Listeners don't like speakers who play favorites, who look with stiff-necked fixity in just one direction.

Look at *all* of your listeners.

### 4. Actually see your listeners.

It is possible for you to go through all the motions of maintaining and distributing contact—without results. What is wrong?

Your contact may be coldly impersonal. It may be so introspective that your listeners could quietly leave the room without you noticing it. You would still swing your head correctly from side to side and look, with unfocused eyes, at your "audience."

Listeners are quick to detect the real from the sham. If your contact is to count, you must look at your listeners as individuals, rather than as a composite blur. You must look at a given listener with friendly, alert *focused* eyes. That listener must say, "The next time this speaker sees me he will recognize me!"

It is not enough that you look at your listeners. You must *see* them as well.

### 5. Maintain an alert body carriage.

No complicated ritual is involved in the development of a body carriage that listeners like.

Merely balance your weight *alertly* on both feet. Let your arms hang *alertly* at your sides, ready for instant action. Carry your center of gravity *alertly* —slightly forward.

Listeners like speakers who, if suddenly struck dead, fall on their faces rather than on their backs.

They dislike horse-in-the-stall speakers who sag unalertly on hind legs. They dislike lopsided speakers who would tip completely over in a light breeze. They dislike flat-footed speakers who look as if they weren't going anywhere. They dislike hand-hiders who achieve composure at the expense of readiness for action.

If you want listeners to like you, tell them by your body carriage that you know their time is valuable . . . that you appreciate this opportunity to address them . . . that you propose to stay on your toes and alertly use all your physical resources as long as you claim their time.

## 6. Make your body behave.

If you are nervous when you rise to speak—good!

It means your batteries are charged.

Nervousness is the penalty you pay for being a race horse instead of a cow.

Your job as a speaker is not to "conquer" your nervousness, but to *use* it, to keep this vital electric charge from expressing itself in the form of distracting mannerisms.

Relax your arms.

Relax your fingers.

Let them hang quietly at your sides until you wish to use them for some purposeful movement.

Poise your body so that it is free from a lateral sway or an up-and-down toe-teeter.

Keep your feet still—except when you wish them to carry you to another place on the platform in a purposeful change of position.

Make sure that all your platform movements are *purposeful*.

Don't be, physically, a desk-blotter scribbler.

Here are some of the "scribble" movements that listeners particularly dislike:

> weight-shifting
> body-swaying
> toe-teetering
> arm-swinging
> finger-fidgeting
> hand-hiding
> clothing-adjusting
> shoe-shuffling

Erase these meaningless mannerisms from your platform behavior.

Make your physical presence a clean tablet for the recording of *purposeful movement.*

When this work of erasure has been completed, you need no longer worry about the handicap of your nervousness. It will be, not a handicap, but an asset.

### 7. Gesture!—Don't gesticulate.

If you are to deliver your speech with the full resources of your personality, it goes without saying that you must use your hands.

Use your hands to describe.

Use your hands to punctuate.

And, in using your hands, observe seven simple laws of gesture execution:

(1) *Start your gestures from the shoulder.*

Listeners dislike the awkward angularity of elbow gestures.

(2) *Lift your gestures well above sea-level.*

Listeners dislike "fish" gestures that flop around in the neighborhood of the speaker's knees.

A gesture well up above waist-level fuses

99

with the rest of the speaker's personality. A "fish" gesture divides attention, pulling the eyes of listeners *down*, away from the speaker's eyes.

NO GESTURE IS GOOD WHICH ATTRACTS ATTENTION TO ITSELF.

**(3)** *Start the upstroke of your gesture well in advance of the word selected for emphasis.*

Listeners dislike startling gestures that dart out abruptly at the last moment.

**(4)** *Make the downstroke of your gesture "click" cleanly on a selected syllable.*

Listeners like crisp gestures that climax accurately. They dislike groping gestures that move around vaguely, reach no particular climax—then fade fuzzily away.

**(5)** *As soon as your gesture "clicks," drop your arm to your side—without an aftermath of flourish or handswinging.*

Listeners like gestures which accomplish their purpose so simply, that only the effect is noted—not the gestures themselves.

**(6)** *Gesture with "live" fingers.*

Hold an imaginary pineapple in your hand when you gesture. Listeners dislike the unexpressiveness of limp, weakly closed fingers.

**(7)** *Gesture with discrimination.*

Beware the temptation to merely beat time with your hands, awarding a gesture to every other word as a matter of routine.

Listeners dislike speakers who hit thought thumb-tacks with gesture sledge hammers.

*HOW TO PLEASE YOUR*
*LISTENERS' EARS*

## 1. Talk!—Don't orate.

LISTENERS of today dislike speakers who "make speeches."

Demosthenes is dead!

If you want to please your listeners when you take the platform, *talk with the same conversational inflections that you use in your home.*

You are mounting a platform, remember, not a soap-box. You are wearing a business suit, not a toga.

When you walk forward on the platform and face your audience, avoid the temptation to strike a vocal pose. Talk—don't orate! Talk sincerely. Talk spontaneously. Talk with simple directness.

The minute you feel a compulsion to orate creep over you, repeat under your breath the following curative phrase: "Now here's the idea, Mrs. Murphy . . ."

That's what your listeners want—the idea! Forget the rock-bound coasts of Maine and the sun-kissed shores of California. Forget the vocal tricks of pulpiteer and politician.

Give Mrs. Murphy . . . *the idea!*

## 2. Talk animatedly.

"Talk conversationally" doesn't mean "talk monotonously."

It means the reverse.

The voice of the sincere conversationalist sparkles with *change*—change of pitch, change of volume, change of rate.

(a) *Change of Pitch*

Make sure that the normal up-and-down movements of your voice are not strait-jacketed by platform nervousness.

The vocal topography that listeners like is animatedly alpine—full of unpredictable peaks and valleys. Listeners definitely dislike the pitch plain.

Remember that absence of pitch variation is the technique of hypnosis, of inducing sleep through the progressive paralysis of conscious attention. As the hypnotist talks to his subject, he carefully excludes from his voice all the normal changes of pitch.

The goal of your delivery is to awaken—not to lull!

You are a speaker—not a hypnotist!

**(b)** *Change of Volume*

In every sentence you deliver there's at least one word that deserves selective emphasis.

Hit that word with the hammer of increased volume. Hit it cleanly—sharply!

Then lay your hammer aside for a few words.

The technique of volume variation means more than knowing when to hit hard. It means knowing when to hit softly—and knowing when not to hit at all.

Listeners dislike anæmic speakers who talk in a volume monotone. But they also dislike apoplectic speakers who cry, "Wolf! Wolf!" continuously—who are unchangingly emphatic.

To provide effective volume highlights, you must also provide volume shadows. *Modu-*

*late your voice.* Learn to use the whispers as well as the shouts in the vocabulary of volume variation.

## (c) *Change of Rate*

If you talk faster than 160 words a minute, you violate the maximum speed law of audience understanding.

If you talk more slowly than 90 words a minute, you block thought traffic.

Since an over-rapid delivery confuses and an over-deliberate delivery irritates, make sure that your average speed remains well within the safety zone.

So much for your *average* speed.

Actually, you should deliver no two sentences with the same rapidity. Your rate, like your pitch and your volume, should constantly change. Never so fast that the average is driven up above 160—never so slow that the average drops below 90—*but always changing.*

Did you ever watch a sight-seeing bus move through a city? As it passes a row of uninteresting buildings it speeds up. When it comes to an important building, it slows down. Occasionally, before a historic landmark, it comes to a complete stop.

Imitate the technique of the sight-seeing bus in your speed of delivery. Give that unimportant transitional sentence with breezy dispatch. Slow down as you state your next key thought. Speed up again as you pile "for-instance" upon "for-instance." Become impressively deliberate as you approach your conclusion. Pause for a half-second before you utter that last climactic word.

Rate change does more than invest your voice with an added quality of animation. It takes its place with pitch change and volume change as a technique of *interpretation*.

### 3. Talk clearly!

Focus your vocal delivery on three members of your audience:

(1) the man in the last row;
(2) the old gentleman with defective hearing in the middle of the room;

(3) the foreign guest in the front row, who doesn't understand English any too well.

Talk loudly enough so that the man in the last row can hear you, without "working at it." Spare your audience the nerve-wracking chore of *paying* attention.

Follow through to your sentence ends with such crispness that the man with defective hearing will catch your closing as well as your opening words. Avoid sentence "trail-offs."

Talk with such accuracy of enunciation that the foreign guest will readily identify your words. Avoid both the sound-unit omissions of careless speech and the sound unit-substitutions of provincial dialect.

If your speech is impaired by an imperfect language transition, an organic malformation, or a psychological impediment, do something about it! Stammering can be treated. Nasality and harsh tone quality can be treated. Articulatory defects of organic origin can be corrected. Foreign accent can be eliminated.

Talk clearly!

## 4. Talk with composure.

The enemies of vocal composure are poor pauses.

Learn the technique of pause and you learn the technique of poise.

## PAUSE PRINCIPLE No. 1

*Make sure that your pauses punctuate rather than mutilate.*

To achieve vocal composure, pause only where marks of punctuation might occur if you were writing instead of speaking.

Use comma pauses at the end of phrases, semi-colon pauses at the end of clauses, period pauses at the end of sentences.

*Avoid nervous pauses after prepositions and articles!*

Such pauses, instead of punctuating, mutilate. They behead groups of words that logically belong together, dividing your thought into fragments rather than phrases. They result, not in a composed delivery, but in an agitated "glug" delivery—reminiscent of the uncontrolled way water sometimes blurts from a narrow-necked bottle.

Learn to pour out your words smoothly, pausing, not at the end of a nervous "glug," but when a phrase cup has been filled.

## PAUSE PRINCIPLE No. 2

*When you pause—pause cleanly.*

The worst foe of vocal composure is the pause whisker—the deadly "ER-R-R."

Listen to a typical er-addict bewhisker his pauses:

> One of the . . . er-r-r . . . most effective ways to . . . er-r-r . . . fight the sales tax is to . . . er-r-r . . . organize in consumer groups and refuse to . . . er-r-r . . . er-r-r . . .

Study this vocal delivery for a few moments and you will discover the psychology behind the pause whisker. The speaker recognizes instinctively that his pauses after prepositions and articles mutilate, rather than punctuate, so he naïvely attempts to cover up these pauses by sound camouflage.

The "er" is the sound sandhill into which the speaking ostrich thrusts his head when he confronts a wrongly placed pause.

If you are an er-addict—which is quite probable—here's the formula for curing yourself:

(a) Recognize clearly that listeners will never like you as long as you "er." If they see you coming, they will cross the street. When you are introduced at a meeting, they will steal quietly away. An "er" may seem a little thing, but listeners loathe it out of all proportion to its apparent importance.

(b) Work conscientiously on Pause Principle No. 1. When you have formed the habit of pausing in the right places instead of the wrong places, the temptation to "er" will automatically disappear.

(c) Don't be content to attack the "er" habit indirectly, through an improved technique of pause-placing. Attack it directly —by sheer will power! Agree to give fifty cents to charity every time you catch yourself "er"ing. Have your friends help you keep score. At the end of a week you will be broke—but cured!